THE
TOTALLY
GARLIC
COOKBOOK

Printed in Singapore

The Totally Garlic Cookbook is produced by becker&mayer!, Ltd.

Cover illustration and design: Dick Witt

Interior design and typesetting: Dona McAdam, Mac on the Hill

Library of Congress Cataloging-in-Publication Data:
Siegel, Helene.
     The totally garlic cookbook / by Helene Siegel & Karen Gillingham.
         p.   cm.
     ISBN 0-89087-725-4 ; $4.95
     1. Cookery (Garlic) 2. Garlic   I. Gillingham, Karen.   II. Title.
TX819.G3559 1994
641.6 ' 526—dc20   94-1217
                                                     CIP

Celestial Arts
PO Box 7123
Berkeley, CA 94707

Other cookbooks in this series:
The Totally Chile Pepper Cookbook
The Totally Mushroom Cookbook
The Totally Corn Cookbook

THE
TOTALLY
GARLIC
COOKBOOK

by Helene Siegel and Karen Gillingham
Illustrations by Ani Rucki

CELESTIAL ARTS
BERKELEY, CA

CONTENTS

If ever an ingredient deserved a cult following, it is garlic. What other food promises to lower blood pressure, reduce "bad" cholesterol, cure athlete's foot, leprosy, cancer, and gout, AND clear your sinuses while it boosts the flavor of just about every food it brushes up against?

Add to that the fact that it is inexpensive, grown domestically, always available, easy to pronounce, and a known vampire retardant and you have a sure winner in the single-ingredient culinary sweepstakes.

Luckily, thanks to those early garlic pioneers such as Alice Waters, Lloyd J. Harris, and the good people of Gilroy, garlic is no longer an oddity in the standard American kitchen.

The authors of *The Totally Garlic Cookbook* proudly proclaim this ingredient's use in sturdy garlic breads, breadsticks and pastas, sinus-clearing broths, fragrant rice pilafs, and bold side dishes of asparagus,

eggplant, spinach, potatoes, and salad greens—
all liberally sprinkled with garlic. Included are a few
garlic classics such as chicken with forty cloves and
aioli as well as some new twists on preparing lamb,
pork, and beef that we hope will stimulate further
garlic experimentation.

Which brings us to the controversial subject of
desserts. Once we were on a (garlic) roll we just
couldn't resist experimenting with sugar, honey,
milk, and our favorite ingredient. The resulting
desserts have an alluring savory underpinning that
may leave your guests dazed and confused—or at
least wondering what they have been eating.
A sense of humor (among the guests) may be
the secret ingredient.

Be forewarned. All the recipes here are
guaranteed to fill your kitchen, palate, and memory
bank with the happy smell of garlic, garlic, and
more garlic. Cook, eat and be happy!

CONTENTS

PANTRY ITEMS & LIFESAVERS

"It is not really an exaggeration to say that peace and happiness begin, geographically, where garlic is used in cooking."

X. Marcel Boulestin

GARLIC SALSA

10 garlic cloves, chopped
3/4 cup chopped fresh Italian parsley
1/2 cup olive oil
   Coarse salt and freshly ground pepper
1/4 teaspoon dried red pepper flakes (optional)
 1 baguette

In bowl, combine garlic, parsley, and olive oil.
Season to taste with salt, pepper and, if desired,
red pepper flakes. Tear baguette into bite-sized
pieces and dip into salsa or serve with grilled
chicken or meats.

Serves 4 to 6.

GARLIC WINE VINEGAR

| 1 head garlic
| 4 cups white wine vinegar

Separate garlic into cloves and peel. Place in heat-proof 1½-quart bowl. In a non-reactive pan, bring vinegar to boil. Pour over garlic. Cool, then cover. Allow to stand overnight. Pour into jars or bottles, adding a few garlic cloves for garnish. Seal tightly and store in refrigerator.

Makes 2 pints.

GARLIC
SEASONING PASTE

18 to 24 large garlic cloves, peeled
2 tablespoons olive oil
2 tablespoons soy sauce
1 tablespoon Dijon mustard
1 tablespoon honey
Dash cayenne pepper

Combine all ingredients in blender and process until smooth. Store, tightly covered, in refrigerator. Use to season fish, chicken, ribs, or hamburgers for grilling; rub under skin of turkey or chicken before roasting; or, add to soups, salad dressings, or pasta.

Makes about ½ cup paste.

ROASTED GARLIC

*Roasted garlic is soft, mellow, nutty, and buttery—
pure heaven for the helplessly garlic addicted.*

6 garlic heads
6 tablespoons olive oil

Preheat oven to 350 degrees F.

Using a sharp knife, cut about ½ inch off
the top of each garlic head. Arrange in a shallow
baking dish and drizzle oil evenly over tops.
Bake 45 to 60 minutes or until soft, brushing
often with oil.

Serves 6.

GARLIC OIL

Before you lay out cash for that fancy bottle of garlic oil, try making your own. Guaranteed to be just as good, and much easier on the wallet.

 1 head garlic
About 3 cups olive oil

Separate garlic into cloves and peel. Place in jar or bottle. For decorative effect, thread garlic cloves on bamboo skewer. Fill with oil and tightly seal. Let stand overnight before using, then store in refrigerator. Use for dressings, marinades, and sautés.

Makes 3 cups.

CONFIT OF GARLIC

5 garlic heads
1 teaspoon dried rosemary
1 small dried red chile or
8 whole black peppercorns
1½ cups olive oil

Separate garlic into cloves and peel. Place in a small
saucepan with remaining ingredients. Set over low
heat for 1 hour. Remove from heat and cool. Transfer
to a jar and cover tightly. Store in refrigerator. Add
cloves and some of the oil to pasta, rice, potatoes or
other vegetables, or spread on toasted baguette
slices. Use any remaining oil for cooking or in
salad dressings and marinades.

Makes about 2 cups.

GARLIC BROTH

Here is a good vegetarian substitute for chicken or meat stocks. Use it as a base for fabulous bean or vegetable soups.

HEALTH TIP

To derive garlic's legendary antiseptic powers, experts recommend a minimum of 12 whole cloves a day—preferably taken raw.

2½ quarts water
4 heads garlic, separated into cloves
1 onion, sliced ½-inch thick
2 leeks, sliced ½-inch thick
2 celery stalks, sliced ½-inch thick
2 carrots, sliced ½-inch thick
1 unpeeled potato, quartered
6 parsley sprigs
4 thyme sprigs
1 bay leaf
¾ teaspoon black peppercorns
Salt

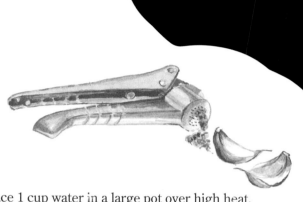

Place 1 cup water in a large pot over high heat. Add garlic, onion, and leeks. Bring to boil. Cover, then reduce heat to low and simmer 10 minutes. Add remaining water, celery, carrots, potato, parsley, thyme, bay leaf, and peppercorns.

Bring to boil, reduce heat, and simmer 1 hour. Strain stock, pressing as much liquid from vegetables as possible. Season to taste with salt. Cool.

Refrigerate up to 1 week or freeze up to 3 months.

Makes about 1½ quarts.

GARLIC BUTTER

A wonderful spread for bread, or try tucking a pat or two between chicken breast and skin or over hot grilled fish or steak.

4 garlic cloves, peeled
1 stick butter, softened
Salt

Blanch garlic in a small pot of boiling water 2 minutes. Remove with slotted spoon.

Slice butter into tablespoon-sized pieces. Mince garlic in food processor, blender, or spice grinder. Add butter and process until combined. Salt to taste and combine again. Transfer softened butter to serving crock, cover, and refrigerate.

Makes 4 ounces.

GARLIC HONEY COUGH SYRUP

It would take a mighty tough cold not to surrender on contact to the curative powers of garlic, honey, and lemon juice. The brandy, of course, helps it all slide down.

12 garlic cloves, peeled and lightly crushed
3⁄4 cup honey
3 tablespoons brandy
1 tablespoon lemon juice

In a small saucepan, combine garlic and honey. Cook over low heat 15 minutes. Stir in brandy and lemon juice. Let stand until cool and strain into jar.

Makes 1 cup.

GARLIC TEA

3 garlic cloves, peeled and lightly crushed
1 tea bag such as chamomile or lemon
1 cup boiling water
Honey (optional)

Place garlic and tea bag in cup. Add boiling water and allow to steep until brewed as desired. Sweeten to taste with honey, if desired.

Makes 1 cup.

GARLIC BRANDY

> 20 garlic cloves, peeled and lightly crushed
> 1/2 cup sugar
> 1 (375-ml) bottle brandy

In 1-pint jar, combine garlic, sugar and brandy. Cover tightly and let stand 1 week. Strain into clean bottle and seal tightly. Use for sipping or in recipes such as meat sauces calling for brandy.

Makes 1 pint.

CONTENTS

SOUPS, SALADS & SAVORY STARTERS

"L'aigo bouido sauvo la vido" or
"Garlic soup saves lives."

Provençal saying translated by John Thorne

POOR MAN'S BOUILLABAISSE

Bouillabaisse without the fish, or Provençal aigo bouido, is a wonderful easy-to-make winter snack.

```
 2 quarts water or chicken stock
16 garlic cloves, minced
 6 sage leaves
 2 bay leaves
1/2 teaspoon crushed saffron
 2 teaspoons salt
1/2 teaspoon black pepper
 4 egg yolks
 1 tablespoon olive oil
 6 slices toasted country bread, brushed
   with olive oil
```

Bring the water to a boil in a large stockpot. Add the garlic, sage, bay leaves, saffron, salt, and pepper. Skim and discard foam from top. Cook at medium boil 10 minutes, uncovered. Remove sage and bay leaves with slotted spoon. Reduce heat to low.

In small bowl, beat egg yolks with olive oil Add ladleful of hot broth to the yolks and beat with fork. Over low heat, slowly drizzle in eggs, stirring constantly to break into threads.

Place the bread slices on bottom of 6 soup bowls. Top with broth and serve hot.

Serves 6.

Culinary garlic, aka allium sativum, is an easy bulb to grow. Simply place unpeeled cloves in the soil, pointed-side up, about 2 inches deep and water regularly. Winter or early spring are the best times to plant and harvestime is late summer or early fall, when the tops yellow and droop.

25

WATERCRESS GARLIC SALAD

Watercress is tart and strong enough to support a shower of blanched garlic slivers and lemony dressi

8 garlic cloves, peeled and sliced
2 bunches watercress, stems trimmed
2 tablespoons lemon juice
1/3 cup olive oil
1/2 teaspoon salt
1/4 teaspoon black pepper

Blanch garlic in small pot of water for 3 minutes. Drain, rinse with cold water and then drain again. Dry on paper towels.

Wash and dry watercress and break into small pieces. Place in bowl.

Mix together lemon juice, olive oil, salt, pepper, and garlic slices. Pour over the watercress, toss well, and serve.

Serves 4.

SHRIMP WITH GARLIC-LEMON VINAIGRETTE

   1 pound large shrimp with shells
   6 garlic cloves, minced
   1/3 cup lemon juice
   1/3 cup olive oil
   1 tablespoon minced fresh Italian parsley
   1 1/2 teaspoons minced fresh thyme
   1 1/2 teaspoons grated lemon peel
      Coarse salt and freshly ground pepper

Bring a large pot of salted water to a boil. Cook shrimp just until bright orange, about 2 minutes. Drain. When cool enough to handle, remove shells and set aside.

In bowl, whisk garlic with lemon juice, oil, parsley, thyme, and lemon peel. Season to taste with salt and pepper. Add shrimp and toss to coat.

Refrigerate several hours, tossing occasionally.

Serves 6.

GARLICKY WHITE BEAN SALAD

1 pound dry cannellini beans
24 garlic cloves, peeled
1 to 2 sage sprigs
1 bay leaf
1/2 cup olive oil
1/3 cup white wine vinegar
2 medium tomatoes, seeded and cho
3/4 cup minced red onion
1/3 cup chopped fresh basil or oregan
  Grated peel of 1 lemon (optional)
  Coarse salt and ground pepper

Cover beans with 6 cups cold water and soak overnight. Drain. Place drained beans in pot and cover generously with cold water. Place garlic, sage, and bay leaf on square of cheesecloth. Gather up corners, tie, and add to pot.

Bring to boil, reduce heat, and simmer 2 to 2½ hours or until beans are tender but still firm. Drain. Remove garlic from cheesecloth bundle and discard herbs. In small bowl, mash garlic. Add oil and vinegar and whisk to blend. Add to hot beans and toss to coat evenly. Cool.

In large bowl, toss cooled beans with tomatoes, onion, basil, and lemon peel, if using. Season to taste with salt and pepper.

Serves 6 to 8.

A FEW OF GARLIC'S BETTER KNOWN FRIENDS:

- *Aristophanes*
- *Hippocrates*
- *Virgil*
- *Charlemagne*
- *Mohammed*
- *Eleanor Roosevelt*
- *Gandhi*

29

CAESAR SALAD WITH ROASTED GARLIC DRESSING

30

How to improve on the already garlicky standard Caesar salad? Try adding a head of roasted garlic to the dressing.

2 tablespoons butter
2 tablespoons olive oil
4 garlic cloves, peeled and lightly crushed
2 cups 3/4-inch French or sourdough bread cubes, lightly toasted
1 roasted head garlic (see p. 11)
2 anchovies
1/2 cup olive oil
Juice of 1 lemon
2 teaspoons Dijon mustard
3 tablespoons freshly grated Parmesan cheese
Worcestershire sauce
Salt and freshly ground pepper
2 heads Romaine lettuce, outer leaves removed
Additional Parmesan cheese

Melt butter with olive oil in skillet over medium-high heat. Add garlic cloves and sauté 5 minutes. Remove and discard, if desired. Add toasted bread cubes and toss over medium-high heat until golden and crisp. Remove and drain on paper towels.

Squeeze roasted garlic cloves to release from papery skins. Place in blender with anchovies, oil, lemon juice, mustard, and Parmesan. Process to blend. Season to taste with Worcestershire, salt, and pepper.

Tear lettuce leaves into large bite-sized pieces, leaving small inner leaves whole. Add dressing and toss thoroughly. Add croutons and toss lightly. Serve with additional Parmesan cheese to pass at the table.

Serves 6 to 8.

GARLIC GOAT CHEESE SPREAD

What could be more Californian than goat cheese, sun-dried tomatoes, and garlic—combined in one powerful little spread.

1 garlic head, top trimmed
4 oil-packed sun-dried tomatoes, minced
3 tablespoons chopped fresh basil
11 ounces soft goat cheese
1 baguette, sliced
   Fresh basil leaves
   Niçoise or Kalamata olives

Preheat oven to 350 degrees F.

Place garlic on square of aluminum foil. Drizzle generously with some of oil from the sun-dried tomatoes. Seal foil and bake 1 hour.

When cool enough to handle, squeeze pulp from garlic. Place in bowl with tomatoes and basil. Mash with fork to blend. Crumble cheese over mixture and stir until well blended. Place in small serving bowl or gather into a ball and form into log about 1½ inches in diameter. Wrap in plastic wrap and chill several hours or overnight.

To serve, slice cheese into rounds and arrange on platter with baguette slices. Garnish with basil leaves and olives.

Serves about 6.

AIOLI MONSTRE

Aioli is the classic garlic and olive oil
mayonnaise from the south of France.

8 garlic cloves, peeled
2 egg yolks
Juice of 1 lemon
3/4 cup olive oil
3/4 cup vegetable oil
Salt and black pepper

Mince garlic in food processor. Add egg yolks
and lemon juice and process to combine. With
drip tube in place and processor on, pour in the
oils in a slow, steady stream. Process until thick
and creamy. Season to taste with salt and pepper
and store in refrigerator up to a week.

Serve as a cold dip with hard-boiled eggs,
crudités, or blanched or steamed vegetables
such as baby new potatoes or green beans.

Makes 2 cups.

EGGPLANT GARLIC DIP

2 eggplants, ends trimmed
  Olive oil
  Salt, black pepper, and cumin
4 garlic cloves, minced
2 tablespoons olive oil
2 tablespoons lemon juice
  Chopped fresh parsley for garnish

Preheat oven to 450 degrees F.

Cut eggplants in half lengthwise and score flat sides with a few deep gashes. Rub all over with olive oil and season tops with salt, pepper, and cumin. Bake on tray until soft and partly charred, about 1 hour. Set aside to cool.

Scrape out eggplant pulp and roughly chop. Place in a bowl. Add garlic, olive oil, and lemon juice. Mix and mash with a fork to a chunky consistency. Adjust seasonings and sprinkle with parsley, if desired.

Makes 2 cups.

PAPPA AL POMODORO

    5 1-inch-thick slices Italian bread
    2 tablespoons olive oil
    6 garlic cloves, minced
2½ pounds tomatoes, peeled, seeded, and chopped
  ¼ teaspoon red pepper flakes
    4 cups water
    2 chicken bouillon cubes
      Salt and freshly ground pepper
    4 tablespoons chopped fresh basil
      Grated Parmesan cheese

Toast bread on a baking tray in 450 degree F. oven until crisp all over, about 4 minutes per side. Set aside and cut or tear into bite-sized pieces.

Heat olive oil in large stockpot over medium heat. Cook garlic until golden and add tomatoes. Turn heat to high, add water, bouillon cubes, salt, pepper, and red pepper flakes and return to boil. Stir in bread cubes and 2 tablespoons of basil, reduce heat to simmer, and cook, uncovered, 1 to 1½ hours, until a coarse porridge is formed. Sprinkle with remaining basil and serve hot with grated Parmesan cheese.

Serves 4 to 6.

TRAVEL TIP FOR GARLIC LOVERS

Southern France and Italy, Spain, China, Russia, and Greece are the best bets for garlic-dependent travelers.

CONTENTS

HEAVENLY
GARLIC
BREADS

*"We don't mind garlic or onions on the breath—
but we do object to the smell of liquor."*

The Lunts, talking about actors and acting

ROASTED GARLIC PIZZA

10 garlic cloves, unpeeled
2 small Boboli pizza crusts
1 teaspoon olive oil
3/4 cup grated mozzarella cheese
1 long, thin slice prosciutto
3 tablespoons soft goat cheese

Preheat oven to 450 degrees F.

Place unpeeled cloves in a small, dry skillet. Toast over high heat, turning and pressing occasionally with tongs until skins are blackened, about 7 minutes. Let cool and then peel. If cloves are very large cut into 2 or 3 pieces.

Place the pizza crusts on a baking tray. Lightly coat each with olive oil. Sprinkle with mozzarella, leaving a bare crust along edges. Top each with garlic, shredded prosciutto, and crumbled goat cheese. Bake 7 to 10 minutes, until cheese is well melted. Serve hot.

Serves 2.

There are 4 types of garlic available nation-wide, the most common being white garlic from California and purple from Mexico. The purple variety has a slightly stronger bite. White or purple may be used interchangeably. The other types are green garlic, which resembles a scallion with a small bulb at the end, and elephantine elephant garlic. Both of these varieties are mild-tasting and should be handled more like a vegetable than a seasoning.

GARLIC HERB FOCACCIA

1 package dry yeast
2 cups warm water
5 cups all-purpose flour
1 teaspoon salt
12 garlic cloves, chopped
2 teaspoons each chopped fresh
    oregano, rosemary, and Italian parsley
    Olive oil
    Coarse salt

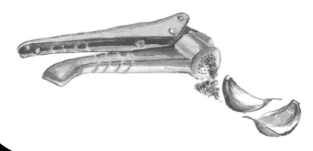

In large bowl, dissolve yeast in ¼ cup warm water. Let stand 5 minutes. Add remaining water. Beat in flour and salt. Turn out on floured surface and knead until elastic, about 10 minutes. Place in oiled bowl, cover and let rise in warm place about 1 hour or until doubled.

Punch dough down and knead a few times. Return to oiled bowl, cover and rise again until doubled.

Preheat oven to 400 degrees F. Divide dough in half. On floured surface, roll each half into 9 by 12-inch rectangle. Place on oiled baking sheets. Scatter garlic, oregano, rosemary, and parsley over surface of each and press lightly. Drizzle each with 2 tablespoons olive oil. Sprinkle with salt to taste.

Bake about 20 minutes or until golden. Serve warm, cut into strips.

Makes 2 loaves.

GOOD OLD-FASHIONED AMERICAN GARLIC BREAD

1 (1-pound) loaf crusty French or Italian bread
1/4 cup butter
8 garlic cloves, minced
1 tablespoon chopped fresh parsley
1/4 cup grated Parmesan cheese

Preheat broiler.

Cut bread into 1½-inch-thick slices. In skillet, melt butter over medium heat. Add garlic and sauté, stirring, for 30 seconds. Brush one cut side of each bread slice generously with garlic butter. Sprinkle evenly with parsley and Parmesan. Place under hot broiler until crisp and golden. Serve hot.

Makes about 12 slices.

To keep vampires in their graves, where they belong, stuff their mouths liberally with garlic before burying and scatter a few extra cloves around the coffin for good luck.

If a vampire does start to wander your neighborhood, a simple garlic necklace or garlic heads casually strewn at windows and doors ought to keep the fiend at bay.

45

GARLIC-FENNEL BREAD STICKS

1 loaf frozen white bread dough
1/4 cup olive oil
8 garlic cloves, minced
2 teaspoons fennel seeds
Coarse salt

Thaw and rise bread dough according to package directions. Preheat oven to 350 degrees F.

In small saucepan, heat oil. Add garlic and fennel and sauté over medium-high heat, stirring, for 30 seconds.

Punch down bread dough. On floured surface knead dough a few times then roll out to about one 9 by 12-inch rectangle. Spread evenly with garlic mixture. Starting at 9-inch end, roll dough up into cylinder. Reroll to 10 by 12-inch rectangle.

With sharp knife, cut dough into 12 strips, 1 by 10-inches each. Carefully transfer to lightly oiled baking sheet. Twist each strip several times to create spiral and sprinkle lightly with coarse salt. Cover and let rise 30 to 45 minutes, until slightly puffed.

Bake until golden brown, about 12 minutes.

Makes 12 bread sticks.

PAN CON TOMATE

1 baguette
1 garlic head, halved across width
2 tomatoes, cut into halves across width
2 tablespoons plus 2 teaspoons olive oil
  Coarse salt

Preheat oven to 350 degrees F.

Cut baguette into 4 equal pieces, then slice each quarter open lengthwise. Arrange bread pieces on baking sheet and place in oven until lightly toasted, about 5 minutes.

Rub cut surfaces first with cut garlic, then with tomato halves, squeezing tomatoes to release juice. Drizzle 1 teaspoon olive oil over each bread piece. Sprinkle with coarse salt to taste and serve with roasted garlic, if desired (see p.11).

Makes 8 pieces.

BRUSCHETTA

Bruschetta, or Italian garlic bread, is a good example of how the simplest food is often the best. We like to make this bread whenever the grill is hot and we have a loaf of bread in the house.

1 large loaf Italian country white bread
    Olive oil
4 garlic cloves, peeled and crushed

Heat the grill or preheat oven to 450 degrees F. Slice bread ½-inch thick and grill both sides until golden and toasty, being careful not to burn. If using oven, spread slices on baking sheet and bake about 4 minutes per side. Brush warm bread with olive oil on one side and then gently rub that side with garlic. Do not overdo it or the bread will taste bitter.

Serves 4.

CONTENTS

GARLICKY
BIG DISHES

"Garlic attracts us through an act of active seduction...Once ingested it suffuses our body with its musky scent, announcing its presence...through all our bodily exhalations, both sweat and breath."

John Thorne

ROASTED CHICKEN WITH GARLIC & HERBS

Here is a beautiful, golden, fragrant chicken seasoned with fresh herbs and plenty of garlic.

1 (4- to 5-pound) roasting chicken
2 teaspoons each chopped fresh rosemary, sage, parsley, and thyme
20 garlic cloves, peeled
1 head garlic
1 sprig each rosemary, sage, parsley, and thyme
1 lemon, halved
Coarse salt and freshly ground pepper

Preheat oven to 375 degrees F.

Work fingers under chicken skin to loosen in breast and thigh areas. Rub half of chopped herbs under loosened skin. Insert garlic cloves randomly under skin. Place garlic head in cavity of bird along with herb sprigs. Squeeze juice of ½ lemon into cavity and insert lemon half. Squeeze juice of remaining lemon half over chicken. Rub remaining chopped herbs on outside of chicken. Season with salt and pepper to taste. Truss, if desired, and place in roasting pan. Roast 1½ hours or until juices run clear when thickest part of the thigh is pierced, basting frequently.

Serves 4 to 6.

53

GRILLED TUSCAN CHICKEN

  2 shallots
  2 teaspoons molasses
  2 tablespoons tomato paste
 12 garlic cloves, peeled
  1 tablespoon chopped fresh rosemary
  1 tablespoon chopped fresh oregano
    Juice and finely grated skin of 1 lemon
 1/2 cup dry red wine
  2 chickens, quartered

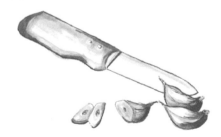

In blender or food processor, combine all ingredients except chicken. Process until herbs are finely minced. Place chickens in large shallow dish and pour marinade over them. Cover and refrigerate several hours or overnight, turning several times.

Grill chicken over medium-hot coals, turning several times and basting with marinade, until crisp and browned, about 40 minutes.

Serves 6 to 8.

CATALAN TORTILLA

Olive oil
3 medium baking potatoes, peeled and thinly sliced
10 garlic cloves, peeled and thinly sliced
1 small onion, thinly sliced
Coarse salt and freshly ground pepper
8 eggs, lightly beaten

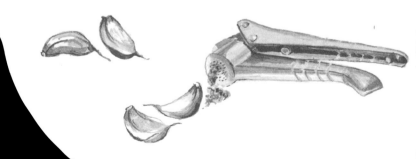

Preheat oven to 350 degrees F.

Coat medium baking dish lightly with olive oil. Arrange alternating layers of potato slices, garlic, onion, and salt and pepper to taste in pan, drizzling each layer lightly with olive oil. Bake 45 minutes, stirring several times. Remove from oven and stir to separate.

In large heavy skillet, heat 1 tablespoon olive oil. Add potato mixture in even layer. Pour eggs over potatoes. Cook over medium-high heat, shaking skillet to prevent sticking. When eggs are set around edges, slide omelet out onto plate, loosening edges and bottom, if necessary, with spatula. Place another plate on top and invert. Add 1 teaspoon olive oil to skillet. When hot, slide omelet back into pan and cook 1 minute longer. Cut into wedges to serve.

Serves 6.

PENNE WITH BROCCOLI & GARLIC

Broccoli is often paired with vast quantities of garlic in the Italian kitchen.

Egyptian slaves built the pyramids on a diet of garlic, bread, and water.

1 pound penne or any short pasta, cooked and drained
1 pound broccoli
1½ cups olive oil
16 garlic cloves, minced
½ teaspoon red pepper flakes
1 teaspoon salt

Trim and discard the bottom 2 inches of broccoli. Blanch remaining branches in boiling salted water for 7 minutes. Drain, rinse with cold water, and drain again. Roughly chop stalks and florets into small chunks.

Heat oil in large skillet over medium heat. Add the broccoli, garlic, red pepper, and salt and cook over medium-low heat 10 to 15 minutes. Toss with hot pasta and serve immediately.

Serves 4.

TROUT STUFFED WITH GARLIC & SPINACH

5 garlic cloves, peeled and sliced
1/2 bunch spinach, rinsed and trimmed
Salt and black pepper
4 small trout, bones and scales removed
Flour
2 tablespoons butter
2 tablespoons olive oil
1 lemon, cut in 4 wedges

Blanch the garlic slivers in boiling water 3 minutes. Drain, rinse with cold water, and rinse again.

Wilt the spinach leaves in a large dry pot over high heat, turning occasionally, 3 minutes. Remove from heat, squeeze out excess water and roughly chop. Combine in small bowl with garlic slivers, salt, and pepper.

Preheat oven to 400 degrees F. Season inside of trout with salt and pepper. Divide spinach mixture and tuck inside fish. Tie with string around center of each to hold stuffing. Dust the outsides with flour and season with salt and pepper.

Melt butter and oil in 2 large skillets over high heat. Fry the fish about a minute per side. Transfer to oven and cook 4 minutes, turning after 2 minutes. Serve hot with lemon wedges.

Serves 4.

STEAMED MUSSELS WITH GARLIC & FENNEL

Another classic combination from Provence.

    4 dozen mussels
1/4 cup olive oil
   10 garlic cloves, minced
    1 fennel bulb, finely chopped
    2 tomatoes, seeded and chopped
1 1/2 cups dry white wine

Scrub mussels and remove beards. Store in a bowl in the refrigerator.

Heat oil in large stockpot over high heat. Sauté garlic for 1 minute. Add fennel and tomatoes and cook over high heat, stirring occasionally, for 4 minutes. Pour in wine, turn heat to high, and boil 6 minutes.

Add mussels, cover, and reduce heat to medium. Cook, shaking the pot occasionally, until all mussels are open, about 7 minutes. Discard any mussels that do not open. Serve hot with crusty bread.

Serves 4.

RUSSIAN PENICILLIN

During World War II Russia ran out of antibiotics to treat its many casualties so they reverted to the original antibiotic: Raw garlic was rubbed on the wounded.

63

GARLICKY SEAFOOD RICE SALAD

4 cups chicken broth
2 garlic heads, halved crosswise
2 cups rice
1/2 pound squid, cut into rings
1/2 pound medium shrimp, shelled
   and deveined
1/2 pound bay scallops
8 mussels, scrubbed
8 clams, scrubbed
1 medium tomato, seeded and diced
1/2 cup diced celery
1/2 cup sliced green onion
   Juice and grated peel of 1 lemon
1/2 cup olive oil
   Coarse salt and freshly ground pepper
1/2 cup julienned basil leaves

In large saucepan, bring broth to boil with 2 garlic halves. Add rice and return to boil. Stir, reduce heat, cover and simmer about 20 minutes or until rice is cooked through. Remove garlic and set aside. Spread rice on baking sheet and allow to cool.

Bring a medium-large pot of water to boil with 1 of the 2 remaining garlic halves. Drop squid into water and cook just until opaque, less than 1 minute. Remove with slotted spoon and cool. Add shrimp to water and cook just until bright orange. Remove and cool. Drop in scallops and cook just until opaque. Remove and cool.

In large skillet, bring about 3/4 inch water to boil with remaining garlic half. Add mussels and clams, cover, and steam just until shells open. Remove and cool. Remove shells, if desired. In large bowl, combine cooled rice and seafood. Add tomato, celery, and green onion. In blender combine lemon juice and peel with olive oil. Squeeze cloves from garlic reserved from cooking rice and add to blender. Process until blended. Season to taste with salt and pepper. Add to rice mixture along with basil. Toss to combine thoroughly. Serve at room temperature or chill up to several hours and serve cold.

Serves 6.

SHRIMP MOJO A AJO

This impressive Mexican dish is perfect for both the inexperienced cook and dyed-in-the-wool garlic devotee.

2 dozen jumbo shrimp, with shells
   Olive oil
   Salt
4 tablespoons butter
4 tablespoons olive oil
10 garlic cloves, cut in chunks
1 tablespoon lime juice
   Fresh chopped cilantro for garnish

Preheat the broiler. Butterfly the shrimp, with shells on, by cutting along inside curve and then pressing flat. Brush all over with olive oil and sprinkle with salt. Broil, shells up, for 4 minutes.

Make the sauce by melting butter with oil in small pan over low heat. Add garlic and salt and gently cook, swirling pan occasionally, until garlic is golden, about 7 minutes. Swirl in lime juice and remove from heat.

Arrange shrimp, split side up, on serving plates. Spoon on garlic sauce, garnish with cilantro, and serve hot.

Serves 4.

SIZZLING BEEF SALAD

GARLIC IN THE GARDEN

68

The next time aphids are attacking your roses try spraying them with a mixture of crushed garlic and water. Watch 'em drop.

¾ pound flank steak
2 tablespoons soy sauce
1 tablespoon rice vinegar
¼ teaspoon Chinese chili sauce
1 tablespoon plus 1 teaspoon minced garlic
½ pound snow or sugar snap peas, trimmed
¼ cup olive oil
1 tablespoon lemon juice
½ teaspoon honey
Salt and black pepper
1 tablespoon vegetable oil
1 large head Romaine lettuce, washed and sliced

Trim steak of excess fat, thinly slice across grain and into 2-inch lengths. Combine soy sauce, rice vinegar, chili sauce, and 1 tablespoon garlic in medium bowl. Add meat, stir and toss to evenly coat, and marinate at room temperature 1/2 hour.

Meanwhile steam snow or snap peas 1 minute and reserve in refrigerator. Whisk together olive oil, lemon juice, 1 teaspoon garlic, honey, salt, and pepper to make dressing and set aside.

Heat dry cast-iron skillet over high heat until hot. Coat pan with vegetable oil. Lift meat out of marinade and cook until seared, about a minute per side. Transfer to paper towels to drain.

Place lettuce and peas in salad bowl, pour on dressing, and toss well. Scatter warm beef over top and serve.

Serves 4.

GRILLED LAMB WITH GARLIC RAITA

Juice and peel of 1 lemon
1/4 cup olive oil
1/2 small onion, minced
8 garlic cloves, minced
3 tablespoons chopped fresh oregano
1 (5-pound) leg of lamb, butterflied
Coarse salt
Garlic Raita (recipe follows)

In large shallow dish, combine lemon juice and peel, olive oil, onion, garlic, and oregano. Add lamb and turn to coat all over. Cover and refrigerate overnight, turning several times.

Grill over hot coals, turning several times and basting with marinade, about 40 minutes. Serve thinly sliced with Garlic Raita.

Serves 8.

GARLIC RAITA

1 (6-ounce) carton plain yogurt
¼ cup sour cream
6 garlic cloves, minced
2 tablespoons chopped mint
½ teaspoon salt

Mix ingredients together in a bowl. Serve chilled.

Makes 1 cup.

QUICK 40-CLOVE CHICKEN

Here is an easy, low-fat version of the classic French country dish.

 6 boneless chicken breast halves
   Coarse salt and freshly ground pepper
¼ cup olive oil
40 garlic cloves, peeled
½ cup chopped fresh parsley

Preheat oven to 400 degrees F.

Season chicken all over with salt and pepper, drizzle with oil, and arrange in single layer in a 13 by 9-inch baking dish. Scatter garlic cloves over chicken.

Cover and bake 20 minutes. Sprinkle with parsley. Bake, uncovered, 10 minutes longer.

Serves 6.

PORK ROAST WITH GARLIC & SAGE

2 tablespoons minced garlic
1 tablespoon coarse salt
1 teaspoon freshly ground pepper
1 tablespoon olive oil
1 (2¼- to 3-pound) boneless pork loin roast
   Whole fresh sage leaves

Preheat oven to 350 degrees F.

In small bowl, combine garlic, salt, pepper, and olive oil. Untie roast and unroll or separate pieces. With sharp knife, make 2 or 3 half-inch deep slits along length of meat. Spread all but about 2 teaspoons garlic mixture over surface of meat, pressing some into slits. Cover with layer of sage leaves. Roll and tie roast. Rub outside with remaining garlic mixture.

Place in roasting pan and roast 1¼ to 1½ hours, basting several times with drippings. Remove from oven and allow to stand about 10 minutes. Slice about ½-inch thick.

Serves 6 to 8.

PASTA AGLIO E OLIO

⅔ cup olive oil
10 garlic cloves, minced
1½ teaspoons salt
¼ teaspoon dried red pepper
1 pound spaghettini, cooked and drained
¼ cup chopped fresh Italian parsley or basil

Combine oil, garlic, salt, and red pepper in small saucepan. Cook over low heat, swirling frequently, until garlic is lightly golden. Place hot pasta in serving bowl. Top with hot oil mixture and toss well. Sprinkle with fresh herbs and serve immediately.

Serves 2 to 4.

YUCATECAN GRILLED PORK

   2 cups lime juice
12 garlic cloves, minced
   1 tablespoon coarse salt
   4 pounds boneless pork shoulder, thinly sliced
      across grain by butcher
      Thinly sliced cucumbers for garnish
      Tomato salsa

Whisk together the lime juice, garlic, and salt in a large pan or bowl. Add pork slices and toss to coat evenly. Cover and refrigerate 2 to 8 hours.

Preheat the grill or broiler. Grill or broil the pork over medium flames about 15 minutes, turning frequently to avoid scorching. Serve with warm tortillas, cucumbers, and tomato salsa.

Serves 6.

CONTENTS

ACCOMPANIMENTS
OR
GARLIC TO GO

"There is no such thing as a little garlic."

Arthur Baer

GREEN BEANS WITH WALNUTS & GARLIC

1 pound green beans, trimmed
Coarse salt
1/2 bunch parsley
1 cup walnut halves
10 garlic cloves, peeled
1 chicken bouillon cube
1/2 teaspoon freshly ground black pepper
1/3 cup olive oil

Drop beans into boiling, salted water. As soon as water returns to boil, remove beans and immediately plunge into iced water. Drain well. Place in large bowl and set aside.

Remove leaves from parsley and place in food processor fitted with metal blade. Set aside ¼ cup walnut halves for garnish. Place remaining walnuts in food processor with parsley. Add garlic, bouillon cubes, and pepper. Process until mixture is like paste. With machine running, slowly drizzle in olive oil. Mixture should be the consistency of thick syrup. Pour over beans in bowl and toss to coat beans thoroughly. Serve at room temperature garnished with walnut halves.

Serves 4 to 6.

GARLIC EGGPLANT

Oil for deep frying
1 eggplant, sliced ¼-inch thick
6 basil leaves
12 large garlic cloves, peeled
Coarse salt and freshly ground
black pepper
Balsamic vinegar

In wok or deep skillet, heat about 1 inch of oil until hot. Add eggplant slices, a few at a time, and fry until browned, about 1 minute on each side. Drain on paper towels. Arrange, slightly overlapping, on platter. Set aside.

In food processor fitted with metal blade, combine basil and garlic with salt and pepper to taste. Process until finely minced. Spread mixture over eggplant slices and drizzle with balsamic vinegar. Serve at room temperature. This dish keeps up to 3 days in refrigerator.

Serves 4 to 6.

IS GARLIC GOOD FOR YOUR SEX LIFE?

Garlic's use as an aphrodisiac is recommended in the Talmud, the ancient Jewish book of law and tradition. There, married couples are advised to eat garlic on Friday night, the Sabbath, so that they may know each other better—in the biblical sense.

As for their friends, the ancient Egyptians, they used garlic as a fertility-testing device. "Let a clove of garlic remain the whole night in her womb...If the smell is present in her mouth, she will conceive; if not, she will not conceive."

Sounds reasonable.

ROASTED GARLIC POTATOES

3 large baking potatoes, quartered
1 tablespoon minced garlic
2 teaspoons chopped fresh rosemary
2 tablespoons olive oil
  Coarse salt and freshly ground pepper

Preheat oven to 350 degrees F.

Cut each potato quarter into 4 wedges and arrange in greased shallow baking dish. Combine garlic, rosemary, and olive oil and brush over potatoes. Season to taste with salt and pepper. Bake 45 minutes to 1 hour, turning several times.

Serves 4 to 6.

ROASTED GARLIC MASHED POTATOES

2½ pounds baking potatoes, peeled and quartered
    Coarse salt and freshly ground black pepper
8 heads roasted garlic (see p.11), peeled and
    mashed
4 tablespoons butter
1 cup milk

In a medium saucepan, cover potatoes with water.
Bring to a boil, add salt, reduce to a simmer and cook
until tender, 15 minutes. Drain and mash potatoes in
pot with masher.

In small saucepan, combine garlic, butter, and
milk. Cook over low heat, stirring, until a smooth
paste is formed.

Turn heat to low under potatoes and mash in
garlic mixture. Season generously with salt and
pepper and serve.

Serves 4 to 6.

SAUTÉED SPINACH WITH GARLIC & LEMON SLIVERS

1 tablespoon olive oil
12 garlic cloves, peeled and slivered
1½ pound spinach, rinsed and trimmed
Coarse salt and freshly ground pepper
Skin of ½ lemon, slivered

In large skillet, heat olive oil over medium-high heat. Add garlic and cook, stirring, about 1 minute, or until just pale golden. Add spinach with water that clings to leaves, and cook just until wilted, stirring several times. Season to taste with salt and pepper. Add lemon skin, toss, and serve.

Serves 4.

GARLIC ASPARAGUS

   1 (14-ounce) can reduced-sodium chicken broth
   3 tablespoons olive oil
  12 garlic cloves, peeled and cut in halves lengthwise
1½ pound asparagus, trimmed
     Coarse salt and freshly ground pepper
     Grated skin of 1 lemon

In large skillet, bring broth, oil, and garlic to boil. Add asparagus and return to boil. Reduce heat to medium, cover, and cook just until asparagus is tender but still crisp, about 5 minutes. Remove with slotted spoon to warm serving plate. Raise heat and cook liquid and garlic in pan until syrupy and reduced to about ½ cup. Season with salt and pepper to taste. Pour over asparagus and sprinkle with lemon skin.

Serves 4 to 6.

RICE PILAF WITH PEPPERS & PINENUTS

2 tablespoons butter
8 garlic cloves, peeled and thinly sliced
2 cups chicken broth
1 cup long-grain rice
1/2 cup finely diced red bell pepper
1/4 cup pinenuts, toasted

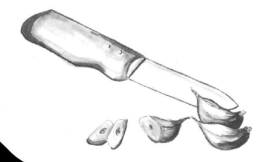

In medium saucepan, melt butter over medium heat. Add garlic and sauté about 1 minute, stirring constantly. Add broth and bring to boil. Stir in rice. When mixture returns to boil, reduce heat, cover, and simmer 15 minutes. Stir in peppers and pinenuts, cover, and simmer 5 minutes longer. Season with salt and pepper to taste.

Serves 4 to 6.

GARLIC IN SPACE

When the French joined a Soviet space mission in late 1986, their menus caused an international stir. The French would not go into space without garlic and apparently the ventilation system couldn't dispel the aromas quickly enough for Soviet spacemen— which led to some interesting diplomatic talks.

CONTENTS

SECRET-INGREDIENT SWEETS

"This is perhaps the most controversial addition to food...We couldn't live without it, and we think we have learned to use it discreetly, for our guests have sometimes been obviously relishing and unawarely eating food with garlic in it."

Irma Rombauer & Marion Rombauer Becker,
The Joy of Cooking

LEMON-GARLIC SORBET

1 cup sugar
1 head roasted garlic (see p.11), peeled
  Skin of 1 small lemon
  Dash salt
3 cups water
2/3 cup lemon juice

In food processor, combine sugar, roasted garlic, lemon skin, and salt. Process until skin is finely chopped. Transfer to saucepan and add water. Heat just until sugar dissolves. Cool, then add lemon juice. Cover and chill. Process in ice cream maker according to manufacturer's directions. Store, tightly covered, in freezer.

Makes about 1 quart.

CARAMELIZED GARLIC

1/2 cup sugar
6 tablespoons water
1/2 cup peeled garlic cloves
2 tablespoons unsalted butter
1 tablespoon brandy

Pour sugar into small heavy skillet, and moisten
evenly with 2 tablespoons water. Place over medium
heat until mixture turns golden, tipping pan and
gently swirling mixture occasionally. Gradually add
remaining water then garlic cloves and continue
to heat 2 minutes. Swirl in butter, then brandy.
Serve lukewarm over ice cream.

Makes about 1 cup.

GARLIC CRÈME CARAMEL

1 cup sugar
6 garlic cloves, peeled
1 head roasted garlic (see p.11), peeled
8 egg yolks
1 (12-ounce) can evaporated milk

Preheat oven to 350 degrees F.

In small heavy skillet, place 1/2 cup sugar. Cook over medium heat until sugar is caramelized. Immediately pour hot syrup into 6 (6-ounce) custard cups. Drop 1 fresh garlic clove in center of each.

In blender, combine roasted cloves, egg yolks, evaporated milk, and remaining sugar. Process to blend. Strain mixture into custard cups. Arrange cups in baking pan and pour in water to half depth of cups. Bake about 30 minutes or until custards are almost set in center. Remove cups from pan and cool. Cover and chill until ready to serve.

Serves 6.

PINEAPPLE-GARLIC UPSIDE DOWN CAKE

For such a silly-sounding cake, this is surprisingly good.

⅔ cup melted butter
1 cup packed light brown sugar
1 (20-ounce) can sliced pineapple, drained
10 garlic cloves, or more, peeled
1 (18½-ounce) package yellow cake mix

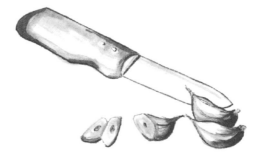

Preheat oven to 350 degrees F.

Spread butter over bottom of 13 by 9-inch baking dish. Sprinkle evenly with brown sugar. Arrange single layer of pineapple rings over sugar. In center of each ring, place 1 garlic clove. If desired, fit more garlic cloves between pineapple rings.

Prepare cake batter according to package directions. Pour batter into prepared pan. Bake 30 to 35 minutes, or until cake tester inserted near center comes out clean. Cool on rack 10 minutes. Loosen edges, then turn out onto serving platter. Serve warm or at room temperature.

Serves 10.

When selecting garlic look for large, hard heads whose paper clings tightly to the bulb. Avoid old heads with greens sprouting out of the top or hollow spots. Store garlic in a cool, dry place such as a potato or onion bin or in open air, never in the refrigerator where it will absorb moisture.

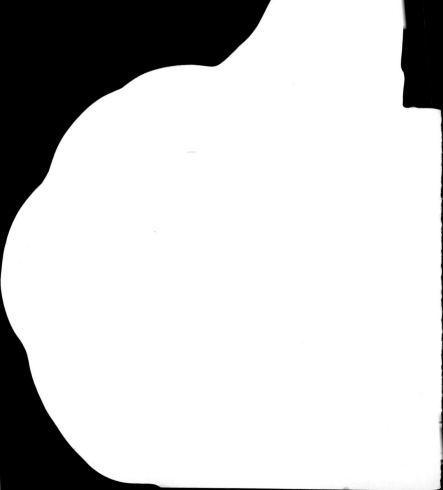